GREAT MOVIES
Instrumental Solos

BATTLE OF THE HEROES

(From *Star Wars*®: Episode III *Revenge of the Sith*)

Music by
JOHN WILLIAMS

21
mf
mf
(◻)
mp
29
mf
mf
3

4
45
Battle of the Heroes - 8 - 3
26249

52
f
ff
ff
3
3

63
ff
68
sfz mp
sfz mp
sfz mp
sfz mp
sfz mp
3
76
mf

80
Battle of the Heroes - 8 - 6
26249

97
ff
mf
ff
f
3
3
3
f
ff
ff
3
3
V
V
p

112
mp
p
121
p
ff
pp
p
ff
8vb

DOUBLE TROUBLE

Music by
JOHN WILLIAMS

Medieval in spirit (♩ = 92)

Double Trouble - 5 - 1
26249

15
sim.
l.h.

28
sim.

38
sim.
48   Driving now, with a "swagger"

STAR WARS
(Main Title)
(From *Star Wars*®: Episode III *Revenge of the Sith*)

Music by
JOHN WILLIAMS

Majestically, steady march ($\quarternote = 108$)

legato
legato
mp
mp
marc.
marc.

21
30
f
f
mf

simile

SUPERMAN THEME

Music by
JOHN WILLIAMS

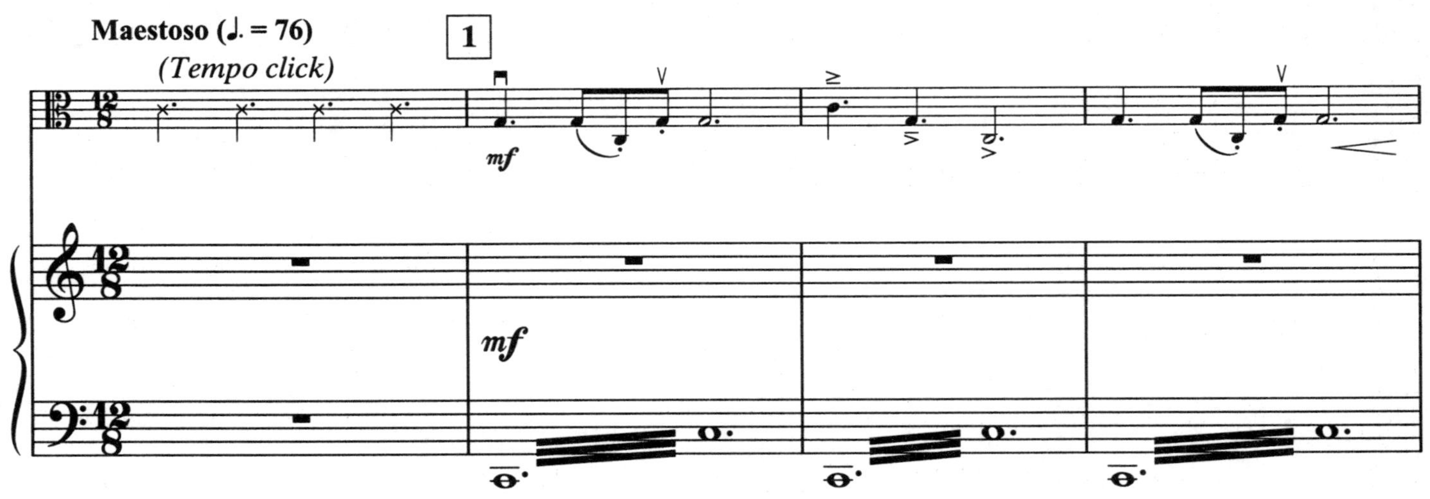

f
f
16
V

mp
mp

32 (♩. = ♪)

46 (♩ = ♩.)

VIOLA
Level 2-3
GREAT MOVIE
Instrumental Solos
CD INCLUDED
Play-Along Tracks with Full Performance Recordings!
INTO THE WEST
THE IMPERIAL MARCH
Darth Vader's Theme
SPECIAL EDITION
LORD OF THE RINGS
THE STAR WARS TRILOGY
INDIANA JONES (Raiders March)
by John Williams
BATTLE OF THE HEROES
(From Star Wars: Episode III Revenge of the Sith)
Music by JOHN WILLIAMS
THE NOTEBOOK
COMPOSED BY AARON ZIGMAN
STAR WARS (MAIN TITLE)
From Star Wars: Episode III Revenge of the Sith
Music by JOHN WILLIAMS
SUPERMAN THEME
by John Williams
DOUBLE TROUBLE
HARRY POTTER AND THE PRISONER OF AZKABAN
Music by John Williams
WONKA'S WELCOME SONG
JOHNNY DEPP
Charlie AND THE CHOCOLATE FACTORY
HOGWARTS' HYMN
Music by PATRICK DOYLE
Alfred

Play-Along Tracks
with Full Performance
Recordings!

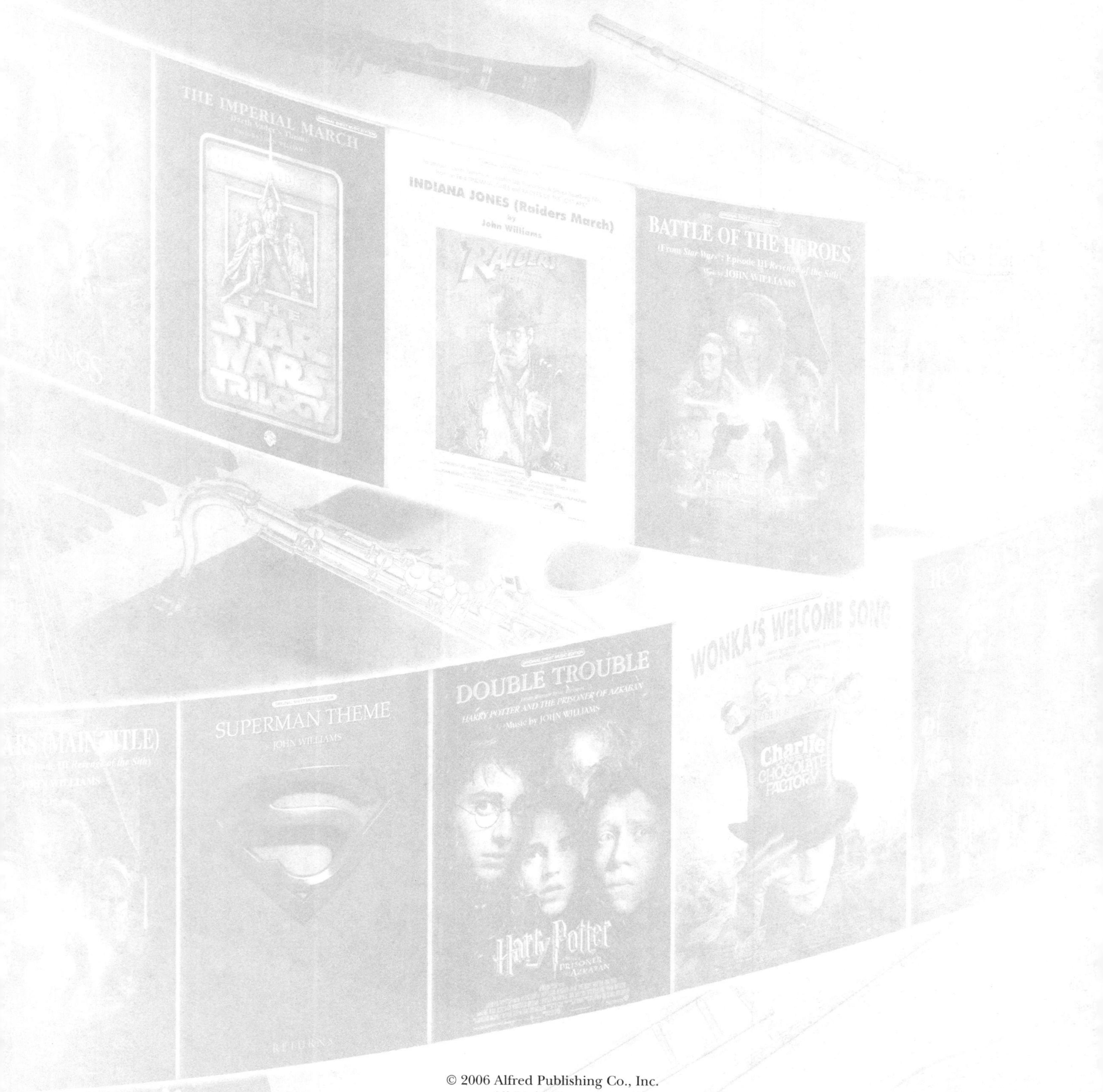

BATTLE OF THE HEROES

(From *Star Wars*®: Episode III *Revenge of the Sith*)

Music by
JOHN WILLIAMS

Maestoso, with great force (♩ = 92)

Battle of the Heroes - 2 - 1
26249

DEMO 4 PLAY ALONG 5

DOUBLE TROUBLE

Music by
JOHN WILLIAMS

Medieval in spirit (♩ = 92)

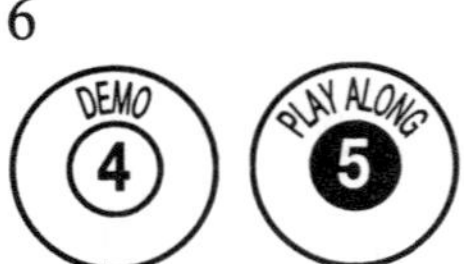

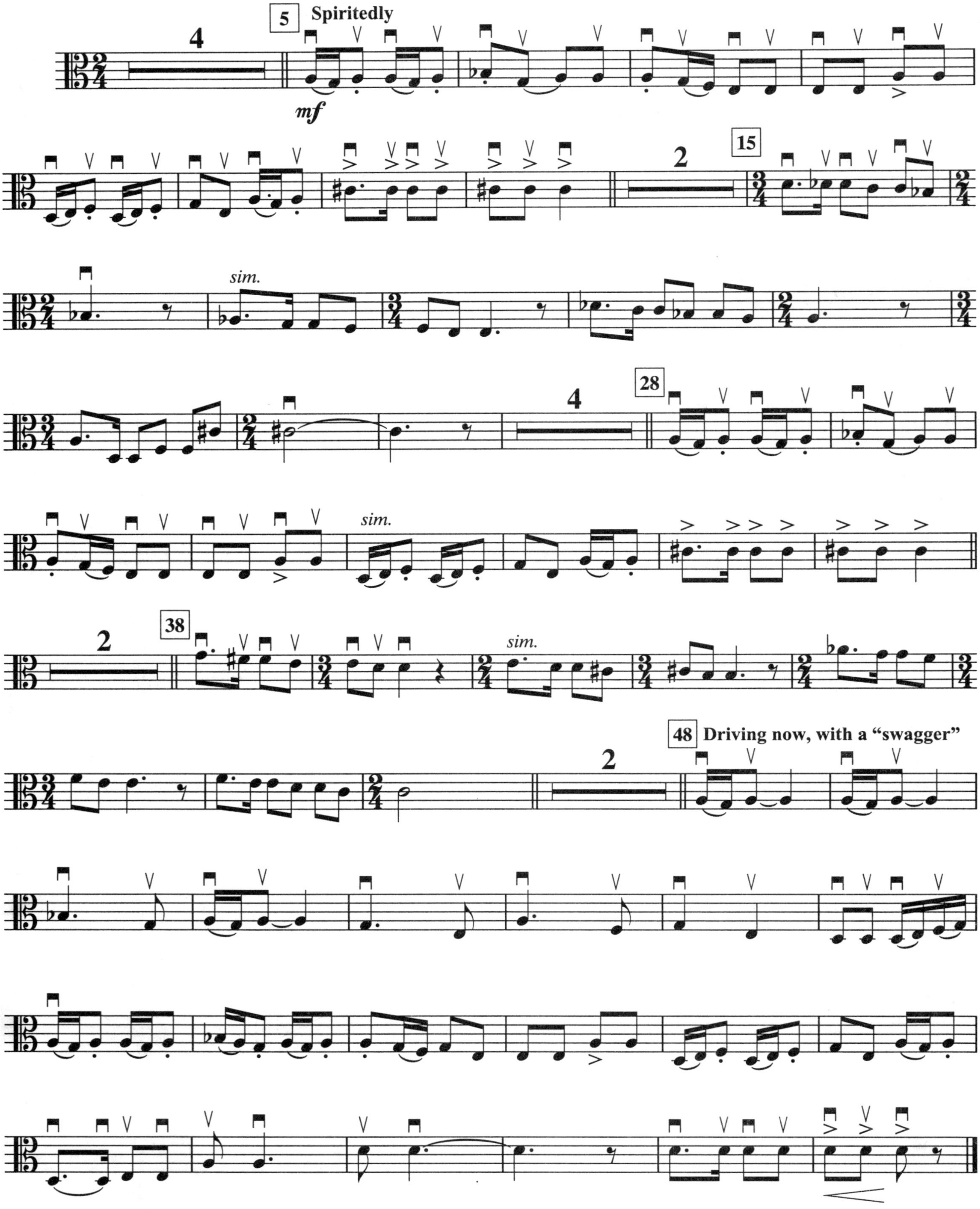

STAR WARS

(Main Title)

(From *Star Wars*®: Episode III *Revenge of the Sith*)

Music by
JOHN WILLIAMS

SUPERMAN THEME

RAIDERS MARCH

34
44
54
cresc. poco a poco

HOGWARTS' HYMN

DEMO 12 PLAY ALONG 13

By PATRICK DOYLE

Noble, with expression (♩ = 69)

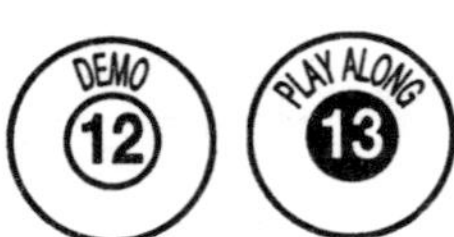

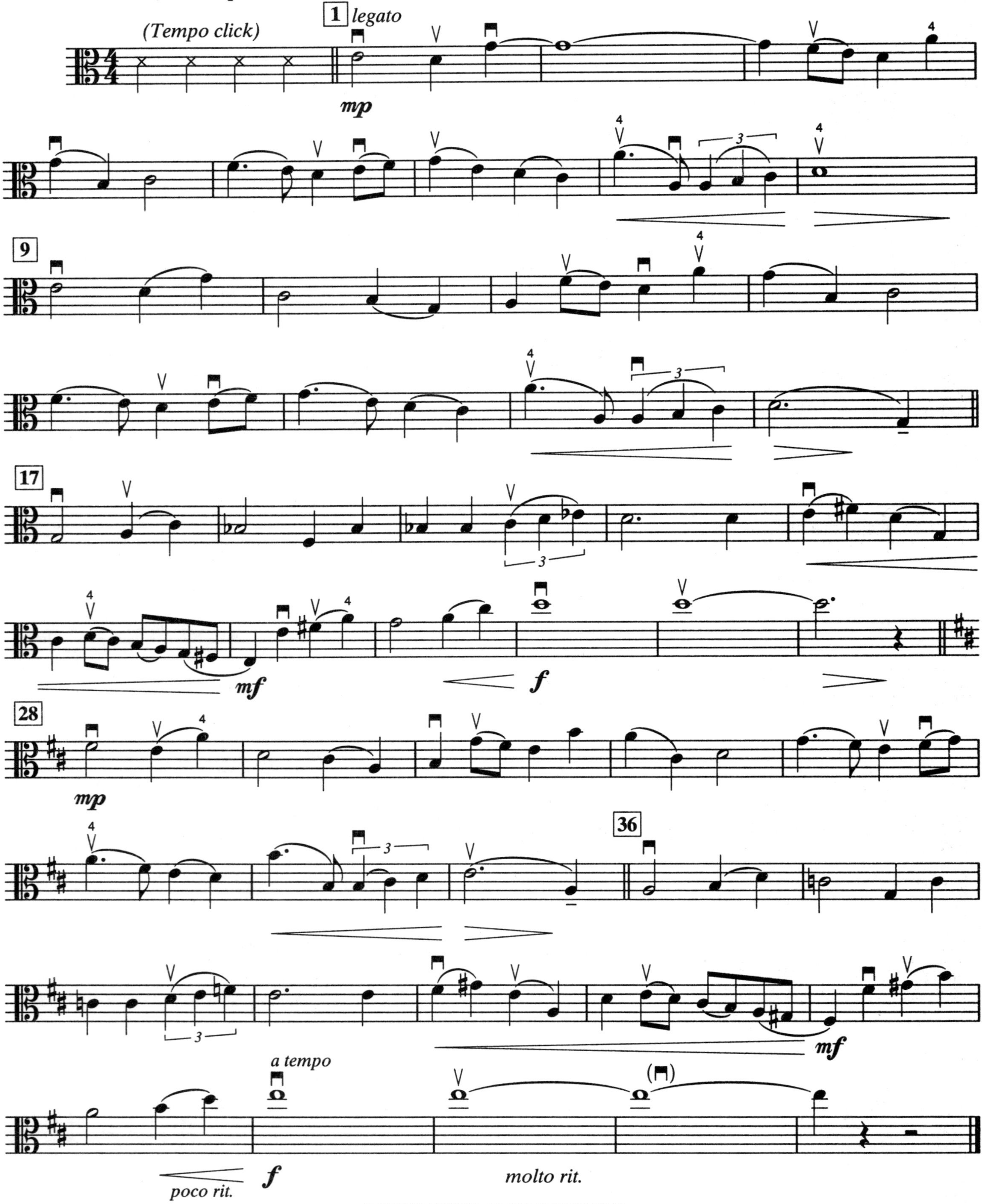

WONKA'S WELCOME SONG

DEMO 14 PLAY ALONG 15

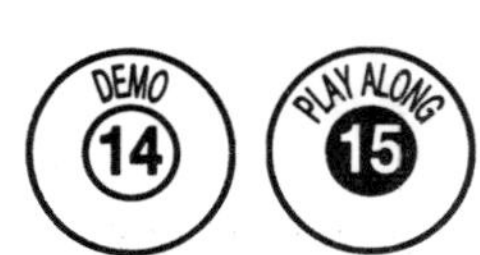

Music by DANNY ELFMAN
Lyrics by JOHN AUGUST and DANNY ELFMAN

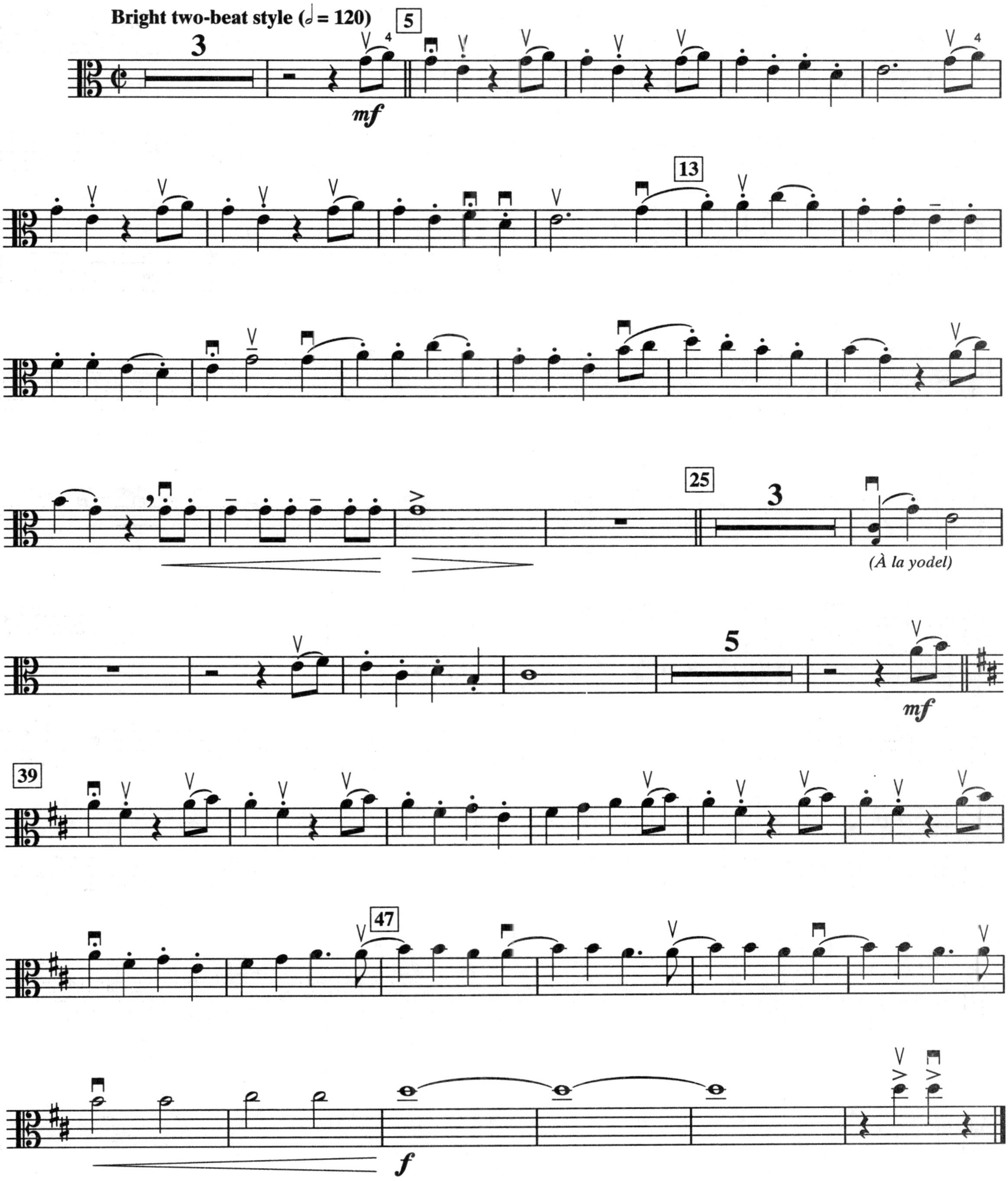

THE IMPERIAL MARCH
(Darth Vader's Theme)

Music by
JOHN WILLIAMS

THE NOTEBOOK

(Main Title)

Written by
AARON ZIGMAN

INTO THE WEST

Words and Music by
HOWARD SHORE, FRAN WALSH,
ANNIE LENNOX

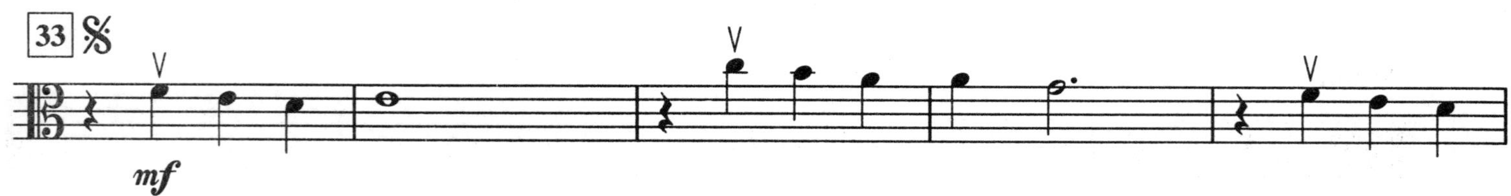

49
To Coda
57
73
D.S. al Coda
Coda
mp
rit. e dim.

This book is part of a String series arranged for Violin, Viola, and Cello. The arrangements are completely compatible with each other and can be played together or as solos. Each book features a specially designed piano accompaniment that can be easily played by a teacher or intermediate piano student, and a carefully crafted removable part, complete with bowings, articulations, and keys well suited for the Level 2-3 player. A fully orchestrated accompaniment CD is also provided. Each song on the CD includes a DEMO track, which features a live string performance, followed by the PLAY-ALONG track by itself.

This book is also part of an instrumental series written for Flute, Clarinet, Alto Sax, Tenor Sax, Trumpet, Horn in F, and Trombone. An orchestrated accompaniment CD is included. A piano accompaniment book (optional) is also available. It includes a CD that features various instrument DEMO tracks from the series. Due to level considerations regarding keys and instrument ranges, the arrangements in the wind instrument series are not compatible with those in the string series.

Alfred
Alfred Publishing Co., Inc.
16320 Roscoe Blvd., Suite 100
P.O. Box 10003
Van Nuys, CA 91410-0003
alfred.com

56

RAIDERS MARCH

Music by
JOHN WILLIAMS

27
20
f
f
mf
mf

34
44
f
mf
mf
f
f
f
f

54
mf
mf
f
f
cresc. poco a poco

HOGWARTS' HYMN

By PATRICK DOYLE

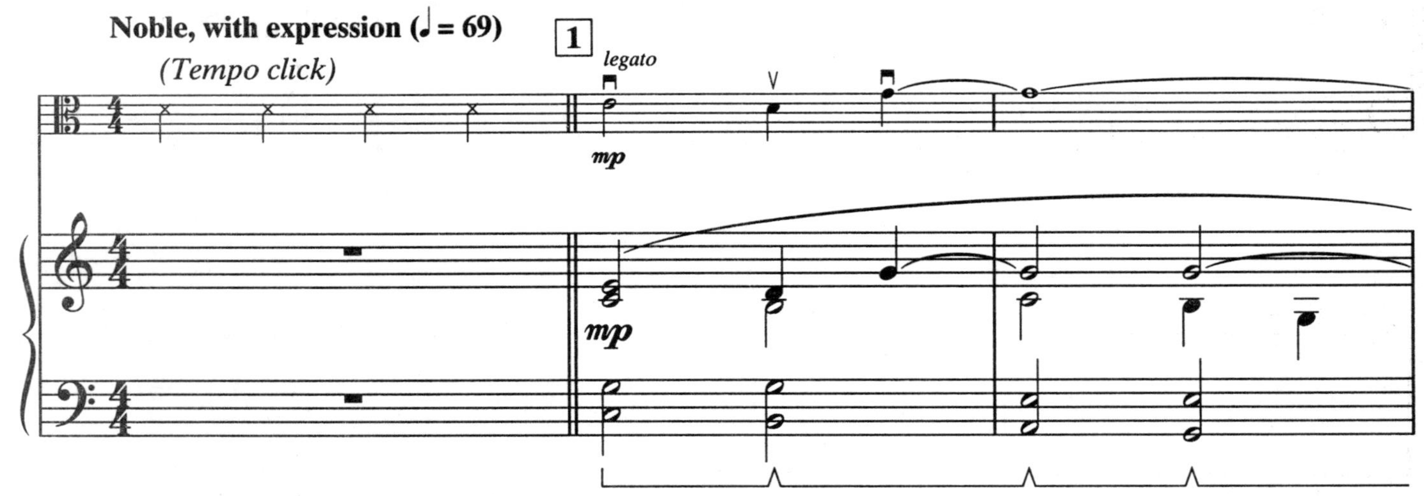

9
17
4

* The cue notes represent more challenging alternative notes.

Hogwarts' Hymn - 4 - 3
26249

36
a tempo
poco rit.
f
mf
mf
poco rit.
f
a tempo
molto rit.
molto rit.
8vb

WONKA'S WELCOME SONG

Music by DANNY ELFMAN
Lyrics by JOHN AUGUST and DANNY ELFMAN

Bright two-beat style (♩ = 120)

Wonka's Welcome Song - 4 - 1
26249

13
F
C
G7
C
F
C
D7
G
G7
25
C
G7
C
(À la yodel)

G7
C
F
C
D
cresc. poco a poco
D7
G7
G#7
A7
mf
f
decresc.
39
D
A7
D
A7
D
mf

A7 D A7 D
47
G D G D G D
G D G A7
cresc.
D
f
f
Wonka's Welcome Song - 4 - 4
26249

THE IMPERIAL MARCH
(Darth Vader's Theme)

Music by
JOHN WILLIAMS

March style (♩ = 108)
(Tempo click)

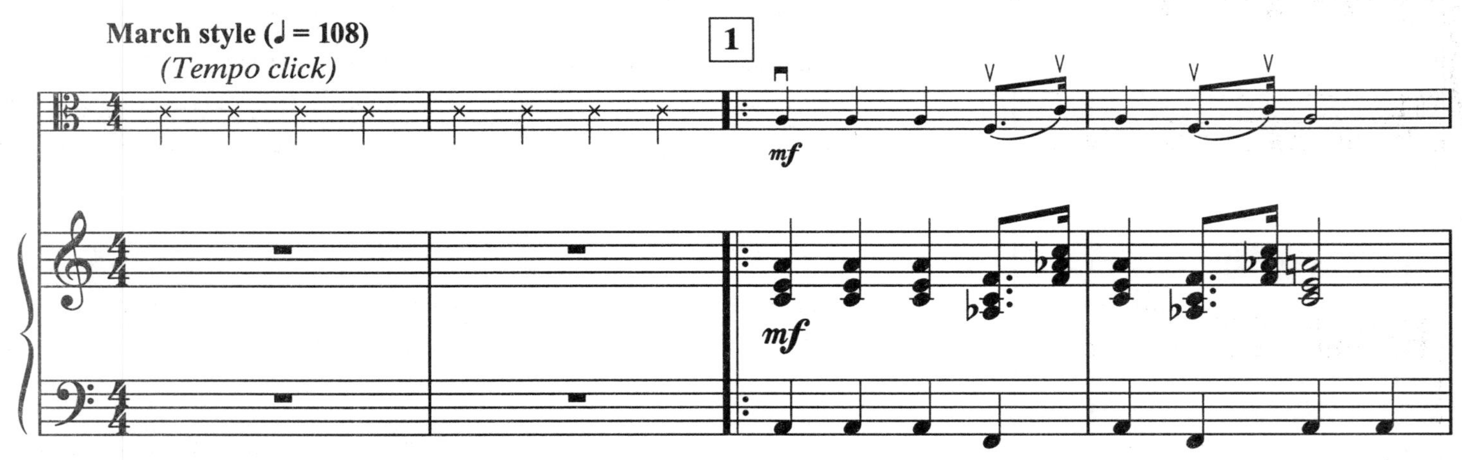

1.
2.
15
mp
mp
1.
2.

20
f
f
8vb loco
8vb

THE NOTEBOOK
(Main Title)

Written by
AARON ZIGMAN

Slowly, with expression ($\quad$ = 69)

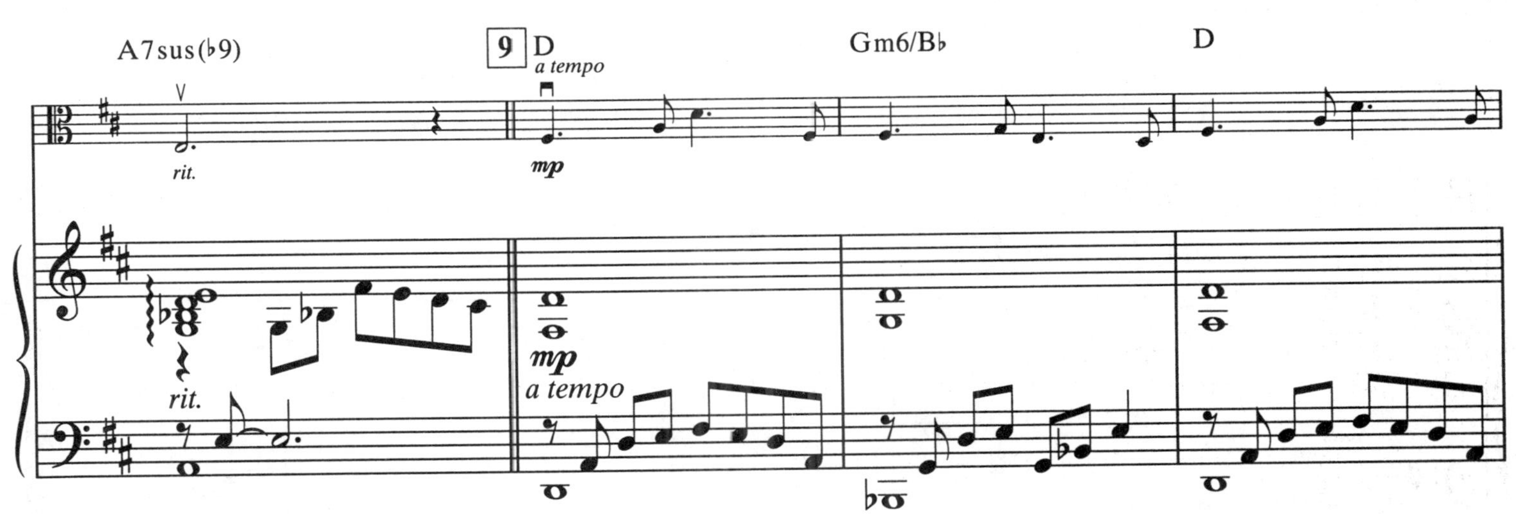

The Notebook - 3 - 1
26249

G(9)   A7/C#   F#m7   G   B7(b9)/D#   Em   Bm7   C
cresc.
mf
mf
Am7/D   D7(b9)   17   G   a tempo   Cm6/Eb   G
rit.
mp
rit. e dim.
mp
a tempo
cresc.
G+   Em   Am11   Am   D
mf
mf
Gsus2sus4   G   C   Am9   Am   D7(b9)
mp
rit.
decresc.
mp
rit.

28
G
a tempo
Cm6/E♭
G
p
p
a tempo
cresc.
C(9)
D7/F#
Gsus2 sus4
B7/F#
Em11
A7/C#
mf
mf
decresc.
34
Dsus
D F#7/C#
Bm11
Gm6/B♭
D/A
A7sus(♭9)
mp
mp
D
D+
Dsus2 sus4
D
mp
rit.
p
mp
rit. e dim.
p

INTO THE WEST

Words and Music by
HOWARD SHORE, FRAN WALSH,
ANNIE LENNOX

45
21
3
Into the West - 5 - 2
26249

33
mf
mf
3

49
To Coda
57
mp
Into the West - 5 - 4
26249

73
D.S. al Coda
Coda
mp
rit. e dim.
mp
rit. e dim.
3